MW01241659

GOD IS HERE
TO HEAL
THE FAMILY

GOD IS HERE TO HEAL THE FAMILY

O.L. Harrison

Copyright © 2020 by O.L. Harrison.

Library of Congress Control Number:		2020923858
ISBN:	Hardcover	978-1-6641-4442-2
	Softcover	978-1-6641-4441-5
	eBook	978-1-6641-4440-8

All rights reserved. No part of this book may be reproduced or transmitted in any form or by any means, electronic or mechanical, including photocopying, recording, or by any information storage and retrieval system, without permission in writing from the copyright owner.

Any people depicted in stock imagery provided by Getty Images are models, and such images are being used for illustrative purposes only.
Certain stock imagery © Getty Images.

Print information available on the last page.

Rev. date: 12/22/2020

To order additional copies of this book, contact:
Xlibris
844-714-8691
www.Xlibris.com
Orders@Xlibris.com
818995

1

I BELIEVE I was about three years old, living in the rural countryside of Southern Pines, North Carolina, with my parents William and Evelyn. My siblings were Liam, Alice, Carol, and Catherine. The air in Southern Pines was as fresh as a summer's breeze. The trees were so tall they looked like they were reaching up to the heavens. The neighbors' houses were miles and miles distant. My parents owned about 120 acres of land. There was always work to be done—milking the cows, picking tobacco, feeding the chicken, washing clothes, and so much more. Every morning, around 5:00 a.m., we would wake up to the rooster crowing and the birds chirping. I remember this one particular day, my mother came in from working the farm; she had not been feeling well for a couple of days, running a fever. Dad said, "Evelyn, go lay down. I'll get the other children to help out when they come in."

When my sister Alice came home, she fixed dinner and prepared me for bed. Daddy was on one side, me in the middle, and Mommy on the other side. I always slept with my parents with my mom's arms around me. Well the next day, I heard a squirrel at the window, and I tried to get up to see it, but I could not get out of Mommy's arms. I tried to wake up Mommy, but she would not wake up, and I could not get out of her arms. I called for Daddy several times before he woke up. Daddy said, "Ruth Ann, go back to sleep," after reaching over to look at the clock. It was around 3:00 a.m.

I said, "Daddy, Daddy, Mommy will not wake up, and I am stuck in her arms."

Daddy reached over and called Mommy, "Evelyn, Evelyn," but she would not wake up. Daddy jumped up and said, "Oh my God," then he pried Mommy's hand and arm from around me. I was really scared and began whimpering and gasping for air. Daddy said, "Go in the kitchen, Ruth Ann, and get some water. Everything is going to be all right."

I did not go, so Daddy picked me up and took me in the kitchen and said, "Stay here for a moment while I call the doctor."

When the doctor arrived, all of my sisters and brother were awake, and Carol and her husband came over. The doctor went into my parents' room to check Mommy, and he came out and told Daddy that Mommy had died in her sleep. I screamed and screamed and cried and cried. I cannot explain how I felt; the pain was inconsolable. I kept yelling, "I want my mommy. I want my mommy."

Daddy grabbed me and held me while saying, "Hush, Ruth Ann, hush."

I felt like I could not breathe; the air seemed so thick. He explained to me that "Mommy has gone to heaven, and when you live right, you will see her again. She is just resting now." I fell asleep in Daddy's arms.

When I woke up, it seemed like I had a really bad dream, but it wasn't a dream at all; it was reality. The house was full of our cousins, friends, and neighbors; they brought all kinds of food over. I can only remember bits and pieces. I remember my oldest sister, Carol, dressing me up and all of us getting into a limousine then arriving in church. Mommy was lying in a casket, dressed up very prettily with a Bible in her hand. Mommy looked like she was sleeping. Someone sang, "Everything Is Going to Be Alright." Mommy's casket was lowered into the ground. Everyone was hugging, and then everyone went back to the house. The days seemed so long without my mother. I felt so empty. The emptiness left me crying a lot. I had nightmares of Mommy a lot.

My sisters took me as if I was their own child. I was never alone because I had my nieces and nephews to play with. Soon the nightmares went away. My nieces and nephews were about my age and, boy oh boy, we had fun climbing the tree for apples and playing jump rope, hopscotch, and hide-go-seek together. I did miss playing doll babies with my mother though. My daddy would always tell us stories about when we grow up. I was Sleeping Beauty and sometimes Cinderella. Daddy said that one day my knight in shining armor would wake me with a kiss and we would live happier ever after.

O.L. HARRISON

2

THE DAYS SEEMED so long without Mommy. It's like life was moving at an accelerated pace. Daddy fixed up one of the bedrooms for me, which I loved. The room was pink, and I had a lot of doll babies. I used to hear Daddy crying at night, but when I would go to his bedroom door, knocking and asking, "Daddy, are you OK?" he would always say, "Yes, of course. I just have a little cold."

At the age of eight, Daddy brought a lady to the house and said, "Ruth Ann, this here is Ms. Estelle Parker, and she is a nice lady. She can cook and love children. She can be a good mother to you. Ruth Ann, your mother would want that for you."

Ms. Estelle Parker reached into her pocketbook, pulled out a lollipop, and gave me one. I told Daddy, "All right," while smiling!

I dropped out of school to go to work when I was in the tenth grade. All my other sisters and brother had moved out, got married, and were having children. Daddy could not do all the chores as he used to, and Mama Estelle, well, she was not as strong as my Mama was. I found a full-time job at a local store as a cashier, and I worked the fields, shoving corn for one of the local farmers when they needed help. I saved my money so one day I could build a house when I got married, and I would try to give Daddy money. He wouldn't take it. He always said, "Save your money for your own future."

I loved to go shopping to buy beautiful clothes, and whatever I wore, I always had matching accessories, jewelry, pocketbook, and shoes. Everyone would say, "Here comes the diva," and that made me feel really good. Just about everywhere I go, people would give me compliments on my clothes and appearance. This increased the level of my self-esteem. On Saturday nights, I would go to the joint where we would dance, drink, and have a lot of fun. I'd get all dolled up. Wow, we could dance the night away as the music came alive.

I met a local man, Paul, and boy, was that turkey smooth. He would dance very passionately, and everyone would say that we looked good together. When we slow danced, he would hold me so close that there was not a space between us. At some point, we would kiss while dancing, almost forgetting where we were. Every weekend when I saw him, boy, he would keep at me, telling other people, I was his girl. Weeks had passed, and this one night when he asked to let us get out of there, I finally said OK. Paul drove to a secluded spot, and we made love in that old Redenbacher car. It was passionate, hard, and good. When he held me, I felt safe and really good. He told me he was married, but his marriage was over and that he had to wait for his divorce to come through, and we couldn't tell anyone because his wife would take everything he had (his wife was my sister-in-law's sister), so I knew what he was saying was true. As I often heard her say, she was divorcing him and could not wait to get rid of "that nigger," referring to Paul. On Sundays, we would go to church. He with his wife and children. (He had two children, the girl, Elizabeth, about four years old, and a boy, Paul Jr., about five years old.) I by myself. After church, he would look at me, and I would lick my lips with a smile. Paul was a lot older than me. I was sixteen years old, and he was about thirty-five years old.

About two months into the relationship, I began to get sick. At first, I thought I had the flu, but then I missed my period. I did not tell anyone. I snuck and went to the doctor. The doctor said I was pregnant. I was so excited because Paul always promised me he was leaving his wife and going to marry me in a few months. Paul always told me he loved me and only me, and soon, we would be together forever (after his divorce). Well, that night, we met at the hotel as we often did, and I told him I was pregnant. He replied, "Shit! I do not want no more damn children."

I said, "Paul, but I am pregnant now with our baby!"

That lowdown, dirty dog of a biscuit said that the baby was not his. I began to cry, and I yelled "WHAT! I HAVE NEVER BEEN WITH ANY OTHER MAN BEFORE OTHER THAN YOU."

He said, "Yeah right," and slammed the door, leaving me in the hotel by myself. I was devastated. I lay in that bed for hours crying and crying. When I pulled myself together, I got on my bike and rode home. I had to go home right then and face my family. I could not face my daddy, so I stayed over at my sister Carol's house, telling her I was too exhausted to ride home. So she called Daddy and told him I was spending the night over her house. They were all being good Christians. I got up the next morning, and my sister had the house smelling good, but the smell of food was making me sick. I threw up in the bathroom and came down the stairs. I told them I had to tell them something important. I began to tell my sisters while crying; they held me and told me it will be all right. They prayed with me, and I asked God to forgive me. My sisters were loving, and yet they did ask me what was I thinking messing with a married man. These married men and any man will say anything to get those drawers off a girl. I told them I could not face Daddy yet, so they said they would tell him and let him know that "you are going to stay with us until you get a place." That was great because I did not want to look into Daddy's eyes and see the disappointment.

As months went by, I did not have anyone to hold me, rub my feet when I was hurting, go to the doctor's appointment, or even just be there for me. When I went to work, people would whisper about me when they came in the store; some were laughing while others were looking me up and down like I was nothing. I told myself that, after I have this here baby, I was leaving this town. I could not believe I was so foolish and blinded I had been. I did have fun shopping for the baby and talking to my sisters about baby names. I did not have to buy a lot because my sisters had had a crib and lots of other baby things from when they had their children.

One night, I was feeling alone. I began to cry all of a sudden. I could hear God speaking to me. I felt God's presence come all over me. Just at that point, I realized that everything was going to be alright. When the baby was born, I named her Isabella. She was beautiful and a wonderful bundle of joy. Her father, Paul, held on to his lie, saying that he had never been with me (even though my baby Isabella looked just like his daughter Elizabeth). Everything he had told me was a lie. It was a trick to get into my drawers like my sisters said. He never intended on leaving his wife for me. I called him every name in the book. I decided, to *hell* with him. I am going to take care of my baby by myself with the help of the Lord. I was so upset with myself for falling into this stupid trap. The thought of staying in Southern Pines and seeing him as he denied our child was unbearable. I needed a fresh, new start. I used to go to the train station and watch other people come and people go all the time. I heard about opportunities and jobs in New York. I finally settled it is my time to move, so I brought a ticket to move to the Big Apple, New York City.

AFTER TELLING MY family of my decision to relocate to New York City, everyone kept trying to give me all kinds of reasons why I should not go. However, my mind was made up, and my brother Liam, his family, and my cousin Sylvia had already moved up north to New York. Therefore, if I needed help, I already had family there. I explained to them that I already had Isabella and my train ticket and that I would be leaving the next day. Then my sister Alice said, "Ruth Ann, are you sure? New York is a little far away and different from Southern Pines."

"Yes, ma'am. If I stay here, I am not going to be happy seeing Paul while he denied our child."

They looked at each other and nodded their heads in agreement. We all agreed that it would give me a new start. Carol asked if I needed any money, and I told her I had a nice savings. Daddy and Momma Estelle came in, and everyone was telling them that I was moving to New York. Daddy came over to me and said, "My little girl is all grown up, and if you need anything, well, home is always here for you, Ruth Ann, and Isabella too."

We all prayed that Isabella and I would have a good life and that God would protect us. Later that evening, I began to pack up our clothes and a couple of toys for Isabella. We had a great dinner; it is as if we were having early Thanksgiving. That night, I slept so peacefully that I just knew that I had made the right decision.

The next day, my family went with me to the train station. Everyone was hugging and kissing me. My oldest sister, Carol, gave me a basket of food and told me to be careful, to always keep my money in my breast, and to only take out small bills when paying for anything. My dad came over to Isabella and me and hugged us; he then reached into in his pocket and said, "Here, Ruth Ann. Here is a little extra money, $1,500 exactly."

I was grinning from ear to ear, telling Daddy thank you. Momma Estelle said, "Let someone else get a hug, Will," while smiling. The train ride was long; the seats were uncomfortable to the point I had to ask the train assistant for a pillow. The scenery was beautiful; the trees seemed to be saying bye as the wind blew through them and the bushes were dancing. I could not sleep, as I was so excited. Isabella was a good baby, not crying the entire trip. When the train finally arrived in New York, I felt a big weight fall off my shoulders. I could now put all that pain behind me—my mother dying, my father remarrying, my first love abandoning and betraying me. The weight of my breakup with Paul was like an anchor pulling me down, *gone, gone, gone*. I promised God I would never mess with another married man again in my life.

I waived a taxi down to go to the Rockefeller hotel. When the cab drove up to the Rockefeller hotel, it was beautiful, and the streets were so clean like the inside of someone's home. The bright lights woke up Isabella, and she was just looking all around. A man came to the car to open it for me, and the taxi cab driver said, "Don't be scared. He is the doorman for the Rockefeller hotel. He is supposed to greet the car and open the door for you, help you with your baggage, and direct you if needed."

I smiled and said, "Isn't that nice." So I gave the taxi cab driver a one-dollar tip and the doorman too. After checking in, I was escorted by what they call a bellboy to my room. When I went into the room, it was genuinely nice, and this was the cheaper room. Wow. I could not imagine what the most expensive room would look like. Isabella and I slept well that night.

The next day, I was up and ready to embrace my new start. I was dressed and ready by 6:00 a.m., so I went downstairs to inquire about a job. The woman said that, well, she was the manager and the hotel always need good maids. She asked me when I could start. I asked her could I bring my little girl with me until I could find someone I could trust to watch her. To my surprise, she said, "Sure." She handed me the application and told me I was hired and to start the next day at 5:00 a.m. I found a church to attend when I was not working. I later met people and found them trustworthy to watch Isabella. On some of my days off, I would visit my cousin Sylvia.

Even though I worked long hours, usually no less than fourteen hours a day for five days a week, I was rarely tired. When I would clean those rooms, I would dream of me living in a beautiful house with doll babies everywhere in my little girl's room. I also would dream of a tall, dark, handsome man that would sweep me off my feet. In my dream, I had the finest china and the biggest kitchen and living room. I kept working and going to Church, but the nights were really lonely. At times, the loneliness seemed like a dark hole swallowing me up. I often thought about how I could have done things differently, but that was just wishful thinking. I remember reading in the Bible, Psalm 147:3, "He heals the brokenhearted and binds up their wounds." I would say, "Please, heal my heart," with tears running down my face like a broken faucet. I guess I was having a pity party for myself. Nevertheless, the loneliness was real.

I remember this one particular day when I arrived to work, a friend of mine, Roberta, asked me if I was all right, and I asked why she was asking. She stated that my eyes looked swollen as if I had been crying. I said, "Well, since you asked, *no*, I am not OK." She asked me what was wrong, and before I knew it, I was spilling my guts out about everything I had gone through. She told me, "Girl, snap out of it. All you do is go to church, home, and work."

I said, "Hold on. I don't just go to church. I serve God."

She said, "Right. But those old—"

I stopped her and said, "Now, just wait a minute. Just because I am going through, that ain't got nothing to do with the church. That was the bad choices I made, and it's what I have to work out."

She smiled and said, "OK, then let's work it out."

I laughed and said, "OK. What do you have in mind?"

Roberta told me about a bar near our job where the men were looking good. So now that we have the place, when and who is going to watch my child while I go out having fun? Roberta said, "You know Tisa? Her daughter Lisa is eighteen years old, and I can ask her 'cause I am going to need a sitter too."

I told her, "No, girl. I better not."

And Roberta told me, "Right. You better not stay home another night alone."

We both started laughing. (I was thinking about church, but the pickings for men were few).

After work, Tisa called me and said her daughter would watch the kids for us. I could let Isabella stay over that night, giving me a well-needed break. Isabella had never stayed a night away from me before, but I knew I needed to get out, so I agreed. I told her that perhaps I would meet a turkey that night. Tisa said, "Well, gobble, gobble." We both giggled.

"See you on Saturday night, but first I have to check with my boss," I said because I was working a lot of Saturdays on call. I checked with my boss first thing the next day, and she took me off the schedule for that Saturday. Having received excellent reports of the service I provided, my boss handed me a letter from the company stating my excellent service and a bonus of $25 and gave me a raise of five cents. I thanked her, and boy, the rest of the week was a breeze. I could not wait to go out that Saturday. I practiced dancing in the mirror and getting all my accessories together. I reasoned with myself, "Well, it has been three years. It's time to really see New York." I told Isabella she was going to stay over at Roberta's house and have ice cream for a snack before going to bed. Isabella was happy.

When the phone rang, it was Roberta telling me what she was going to wear. She said she was going to squeeze into the tightest jeans she could find. We both giggled, and I told her, "Well, mines might not be jeans, but they sure are going to be tight."

When Saturday night came, I took Isabella over to Roberta's house. When I left, she was having some ice cream and cookies, and Lisa said, "The kids would be in the bed by 9:00 p.m." She would read the kids a book about Humpty Dumpty. Roberta, Tisa, and I were off to the bar. Since the bar was only like three blocks away, we walked, laughed, and talked about what if we meet a guy and how to be sure we are safe.

4

WOW. THERE WERE great anticipation and excitement in every step as we drew closer and closer to the bar. My heart was racing. We were about one block away, and we could hear the music. I began to dance while going to the bar. Tisa said, "OK, Ruth Ann you have some moves, girl," with them joining in.

We were laughing, and Roberta said, "I don't know about the other girls at the bar tonight, but we are all coming home with a turkey."

Tisa said, "What?"

I replied, "A man fool with all of us," laughing some more.

When we arrived at the bar, we got a table and ordered some drinks. Wow. That place was jumping; the music was sounding good. I was tapping my feet, and one of the girls said, "Ruth Ann, that man is staring at you." I looked, and he was tall, dark, handsome with wavy black hair. So I looked at him with dreamy eyes and slowly licked my lips. Before I knew it, he was heading my way. He asked me if I would like to dance. I said, "Sure, I thought you would never ask." He just smiled. His smile was like the morning sun, bright yet warm. His shoes were so shiny that you could see the reflections of your face in them. Yes, he could dance. We danced together most of the night. We later sat down, and he asked me now lovely lady what is your name? I replied Ruth Ann. He looked at me as if he was struck by lightning, pausing for a really, really long moment, smiling and laughing. He said, "Well, my name is William and I believe I am the luckiest man in this here bar tonight."

I said, "What do you mean, mister?"

"You are the most beautiful lady I've seen in a long, long while." We both laughed, and he asked, "Where are you from, Ruth Ann?" I told him I was from Southern Pines, North Carolina. "What brought you to the Big Apple?"

I told him, "Well, I left Southern Pines because my mother had died, my papa remarried, and well I, got knocked up by a married man who disowned our child and me." I also told him the embarrassment and hurt was too great (I began to hold my head down while telling him).

William gently touched my chin and said he understood. "Now all of that is behind you now."

I said, "You are damn straight. I felt safe with him, and we talked until the bar was closing. I glanced at his hands, no wedding ring and no signs that he previously had one on, so I asked him if he were married and explained to him I vowed to God to never mess with another married man again in my life. He stated, "No, little darling. Now would I be out here with you if I had a wife at home?"

We both laughed, and I replied, "You would not just be saying that now, would you, Mister?"

He said no. "Now, in these here parts, most people call me Will." He called for a waiter and ordered a couple of drinks. When he paid the waiter, he had a roll of money. Then he asked me if he could call me Ann. I said sure.

At that time, my friends were leaving. Will grabbed my hand and asked me to stay a little longer; he would take me home. I hesitated for a moment, but when I looked into his big, dreamy eyes, I melted and said OK before I even realized I was saying OK. We talked and talked as if we had known each other for years. The bar was closed, and the man was cleaning up. Will took me home. He had a really nice car, so I was extremely impressed. He told me he worked for a printing company. I felt like Cinderella. My prince had come to rescue me, and we would live happier ever after.

When we arrived at the hotel, he picked me up in his arms and whispered in my ear, "Don't be scared. I am really gentle."

Will was very passionate inside my room. As he began to unbutton my pants, I grabbed his hands and said at some point, "You will have to pull it out because I do not have any birth control." He said OK. Will was gentle; he made my very fingertips tingle. Afterward, while kissing me, he said, "Ann, I know we just met, but I know what I want and more than anything. I want you," stating to me that I was amazing.

He began to tell me that he had money and that he would take my daughter Isabella as his own child. 'Wow.' I could not believe it; I met a really nice man.

I told him, "Now, slow down, Will. Let us really get to know each other before we make a commitment like that."

He said he had enough sense to know that "you, Ruth Ann, are what I want for the rest of my life." Will was about forty-five years old. I said one day at a time (while quietly praying) I was about twenty years old.

5

THE NEXT FEW weeks were amazing. Will took to Isabella as if he was her biological father, and she just loved him. I had to pinch myself to be sure I was not dreaming. Could it be that my dreams were coming true? Will would always bring me jewelry, flowers, candy, or something for Isabella; we had an amazing time together. Will would always check with me and have plans to take Isabella and me to visit the zoo, the Empire State Building, the Statue of Liberty, the library, and we often just walked in the park while holding my hand. We had found an ice cream parlor that Isabella loved, and after a nice walk, we would stop in the parlor for ice cream and some peanuts. My girlfriends would tease me and say, with us always laughing, "What time is your husband coming over?" All the loneliness and despair I had previously endured was erased from my heart and was filled with happiness, joy, peace, hope, love, and great expectation.

Four months later, I began to get sick. I thought I had the flu because I could not hold anything down. Will would rub my feet and say, "You have been working too hard, and you need to rest." This went on for about three weeks, and when my period did not come, then I got concerned, so I made an appointment to see the doctor. I was knocked up again (pregnant). I couldn't stop crying because I was not ready for another baby and did not want to bring another child into this world without a husband and father for my child. I told Roberta, and she said she knew a midwife who can help me get rid of the baby. I asked her, "You mean kill the baby?"

She said, "Girl, whatever! You know men say just about anything to get some pussy. Didn't Isabella's father teach you that much! The Rockefellers let Isabella to work with you, but another baby. Come on. Be real, Ruth Ann."

I sighed then I said, "Take me to that midwife." I was fooled once, but I won't be fooled twice. Roberta told me the cost would be $25 for the procedure. I agreed, and she called the woman. She told me the woman had an opening right then, so I said, "Let's go."

6

ROBERTA AND I caught a taxi to the place. As we were on our way there, all I could think about what I had gone through with Isabella's father. We arrived at a building that looked abandoned. When we went inside, there were other girls there waiting to see the midwife too. A lady came out to talk to me and told me that I must not tell any authorities about this place or about her because, if they found out, she would not be able to help other girls. She also said that if she found out that I told, she would be sure that others would kill me. I looked at her, and I was not scared because Roberta said she had gone to her before, and it was safe. The woman then gave me some stuff and said, "Drink this." She would be back to come and get me in about fifteen minutes. She also explained that I might feel some cramps. When she came back to get me, she asked had I had any cramps, I said, "A little," and then we proceeded to go to a room. In the room, she told me to get on the table and to only undress from my waist down. The table was cold, and she put her hands up my vagina. She asked me if I felt that, and I said, "No, just a little pressure." Then she put a cold instrument inside me, twisting it, and pulling. Then a lot of blood came out, and big clogs of flesh came out of me. When the midwife was finished, I had to wait about thirty minutes to be sure everything was OK. She told me that if there were complications, they should put me in a taxi and send me to the hospital. She checked me again and said I was OK and that I would need to rest for a day, but I would be fine. I would be on my period for the normal time of three to five days.

Roberta and I left. We had to walk about a block from the place to flag down a taxi around the corner. When I arrived home, Will met me at the door, asking me what the doctor said.

"I have a bug or something, but I feel a lot better now, but I need some rest and I am on my period, and I still feel a little weak," I said.

Will told me he could stay the night to watch Isabella, and he could sleep on the couch. I agreed. (As Will was old-fashioned, and men did not sleep with women when they were on their cycle, as women were unclean during this time). That night, I was in so much pain bleeding, even feeling weak. At 10:20 p.m. that night the bed was soaked and I was lying in a pool of blood, in pain, and very weak, so I called for Will. And he said, "What's wrong, Ann?"

I said, "I am bleeding like running water, and I am having excessive pain in my stomach," showing him the soaked bed of blood.

He said, "Oh my God," and turned to call the ambulance and my cousin Sylvia. I had to tell him what I had done. He said, "Oh my God! Ruth Ann, what have you done? I told you how I felt about you." Then he said, We just need to get you to the hospital. As he was praying the Lord's Prayer. Our Father who art in Heaven hallowed be thy name. Thy kingdom come, thy will be done, on earth as it is in Heaven. Give us this day our daily bread and forgive us our trespasses, as we forgive those who trespass against us. Lead us not into temptation but deliver us from evil. For thine is the kingdom, the power and the glory, forever and ever. Amen.

The ambulance arrived, and they rushed me to the hospital as I was losing blood excessively, and I had passed out in the ambulance. When the ambulance arrived at the hospital, I was unconscious. Will signed all the paperwork, and they gave me IV, blood, and oxygen. They stopped the bleeding, and the doctor said they were going to have to keep me for observation. About that time, I was awake. The doctor announced to Will that the baby and I were fine.

I was speechless, but Will had this big smile on his face. Will just hugged and kissed me and kept on even rubbing my stomach. He fell on his knees and said with tears running down his face, "Ruth Ann, will you marry me? Wait before you answer. Now I know you have been through a lot, but I want you to know that I love you from the first time I saw you."

Will was crying, and I was crying, saying, "Yes yes yes. Oh, yes!" while gasping for air. The doctor said that both the baby and I were still in danger, but he was hopeful that we both would recover. The doctor and the nurses were clapping and congratulating us.

Will left to call my cousin Sylvia and my daughter Isabella to let them know all was well, and we were going to have a baby and that he had proposed to me, and we were going to get married. That night, Will stayed with me; however, he had to go to work the next morning. I had to stay in the hospital for almost five days.

7

MONTHS PASSED AND the planning of the wedding was extremely exciting and exhausting. I believe I have organized everything because I went to the library and read up on how to plan a wedding. We did not want a wedding planner to save money, so I had to do it myself with help from friends and family. We were going to have to look for a place to live, and I would be out of work for at least two months. The baby was beginning to show, so finding a wedding dress was a little challenging. My sister Carol called and told me she had a wedding dress for me, and it was our mother's. I began to cry because I was happy. She said the dress was a size 12, and that was the size I needed. My other sister, Alice, said she had some accessories. My dad called and said he was so happy for me and that he was going to give Will and me a piece of land, ten acres, for a wedding gift.

Will and I were glad for the gift but decided that we were not going to move back to Southern Pines. I cannot even remember the actual day, but I remember the weather was beautiful and the sky was a beautiful powder blue. We married at my cousin Sylvia's house. Everyone said I was glowing. I am not sure if it was God, me, or the baby, but it was there. I stood outside the door, and Cousin Sylvia was my matron of honor. I reckon her husband was Will's best man, Big Lue. Isabella was the flower girl, and Tisa's son the ring bearer.

When I came in, Will was standing at the end of the hallway with a charming smile on his face. (The aisle was only about 8 to 12 feet long.) My job gave me the day off and some flowers for the wedding. Everyone had been so nice. The living room was set up with chairs, and the kitchen had food everywhere. The cake was a three-layer yellow with white icing, brought from a local bakery, a gift from my brother Liam. My sisters had come up, and they did all the cooking, and man, oh, man, could those girls cook.

After the wedding ceremony, we took pictures of the wedding party, pictures cutting the cake, and of Will and I eating a piece of cake together. We had dancing and toasting. I only took a sip of the champagne. My sweet Will toasted, "May our future together shine as bright and beautiful as you look today, Ruth Ann."

Everyone said "Aw."

The hotel was at the Rockefellers hotel where I was not cleaning this day or imagining I was living out my dream in the best hotel in town. My manager gave us the honeymoon suite, and if you have never been to the Rockefellers hotel in the honeymoon suite, you are truly missing an *awesome* experience. The beautiful crystal chandeliers, the scenery from the big open balcony overlooking the city. The bed was beautiful with red rose petals. There were petals from the door to the bedroom, a bottle of champagne, and even the bathroom was beautiful with white plush towels while the tub was filled with warm water with bubbles and his and hers' white slippers and robes. We brought some food from the reception, and I set up the table. The Rockefellers left us a note and told us not to rush for a place; that we could live there for a year, giving us time to find a nice place.

8

A S TIME WENT on, Will and I became increasingly excited about the planning of our future. One night, about five months later, I was dancing around the room, singing, "Will, we are going to have a beautiful house, and in each room the finest of furniture, china, and linen. Our children are going to go to the best schools, and we are going to be outstanding people in the community."

Will laughed and said, "Now slow down here, Ann. You are forgetting the pool in the backyard."

I had stopped dancing with my hands on my hip. Then I began to laugh again. As weeks passed, Will started to get off work later and later. He always explained that his boss needed him to do some extra work, and he wanted to work more with the baby coming and all.

One day, while Will was at work and I was at work, I started having premature labor pains (eight-month pregnancy). The pain was so bad, I had to leave work and go to the doctor. It was around 5:00 p.m. that evening, so I called Will at his job. To my surprise, they stated he was not there. That he had left at his regular time, 4:00 p.m.

"Ooooooh wee!" I was so mad that, if I were a dragon, I could have spit fire. I caught a taxi to the doctors office, and they took me in immediately. After the examination, the doctor said I was going to have to stay off my feet and that the baby and I could be in danger. The doctor wanted to put me back in the hospital; however, I assured the doctor that I had a good support system at home, and I would stay off my feet, so the doctor agreed with me. "You have to stay off your feet." I said OK.

That night, I went home and got in bed, but I was so mad, I just sat in the chair. Will came home about 10:30 p.m. that night when he came into the room and cut the light on, I called his name out loud, "WILL." He jumped.

He said, "Ann, you scared the hell out of me."

I said, "I called your job tonight because I had to leave work early due to having pains and go to the doctor, but to my surprise, you were not there. Where were you, Will?"

"Hush now, Ruth Ann. I went to the bar with a couple of the guys to get a drink. Girl, you know you are my everything."

I sighed and explained what the doctor said, and Will said, "OK. I got this." I sighed again with a sense of relief but then I told him, "Will, don't ever lie to me 'cause my daddy said, 'If you start a lie, then you will have to live a lie,' and ain't no liar going to see God."

"I've been waiting a long, long time to get the lady of my dreams, and ain't no way in hell I'm going to mess this up. Girl, you have the best stuff I have ever had in my life (while touching me)."

I told him, "Yeah right."

Will said, "OK, Ruth Ann, let's go to bed. I am sorry that I upset you" while rubbing my stomach. How's our baby?"

"OK. We both need some rest."

Will said for me to stay off my feet, that he would see if Cousin Sylvia could help out until he got off work. "Ann, I am trying to get in good with my boss, so please understand. I might have to work some late nights. Is it OK that I go out with the fellas some time?"

I replied, "Sure and after I have this here baby then we both can go out sometimes you with the fellas and me with the girls.

Will replied, "OK, Ann. I won't go out with the fellas and you won't go out with the girls, as we are married now. If you go out, then so will I. Will said so."

"I guess I won't be going out because I sure don't want you going out" Then saying, "Well, I guess that habit is broken tonight."

And I said, "I guess it is."

9

A MONTH LATER, it was time for the baby to be born. Will had stopped going out with the fellas (so he said), coming straight home every night. Will often would rub my stomach and feet while telling Bible stories to Isabella and me. Every night, I would sing us to sleep. What could I do, you know, if it wasn't for the Lord? Well, he's my bread; he's my water, my life, my everything. What could I say, you know, if it wasn't for the Lord?

On August 28, 1955, at 4:00 a.m. while sleeping, a pain hit me and woke me up. I lay there for a moment, looking at the clock. Then another pain came at eight minutes apart; that made me sit up in the bed. I started watching the clock to see how far the contractions were coming. At 5:00 a.m. I woke up Will and told him it was time. He said, "Time for what?" still half asleep.

I said, "Time for the baby to come."

He jumped up and said, "Are you sure?" while another contraction was coming, and I began to breathe really heavily. Will said, "It's time," while calling Cousin Sylvia, making plans for her to get Isabella and calling his job. He told Cousin Sylvia to meet us at the hospital because we could not wait. "This baby is coming."

Upon arrival to the hospital, Will came in the back with me, but he did not stay, being old-fashioned. While at the hospital, at around 9:00 a.m., an ambulance came. They were rushing a lady into the back. The lady with her was requesting to go back with her mother; however, the clerk stated she could not yet. The doctors needed to try and stabilize her, and they needed some information about her mother. At this time, Will had gone downstairs to get some coffee, and he overheard a woman's voice, as she was registering her mother. And she said her mother's name was Ruth Ann Richardson. He walked over and said, "Ava, what happened?"

She jumped out of the seat and was crying, "Mommy was in a bad accident. The car hit her." She also stated that her mother was really hurt, blood coming out of her mouth, and was unconscious. She sniffed and said, "Daddy, how did you get here so fast and who told you?"

He said, "Never mind that." Then talking to the clerk, asking to go back and see her, the clerk said she would check with the nurse. The clerk came back and said, "No, sir. You cannot go back yet. The doctors are trying to stabilize her."

Ava was very upset as Will told her to calm down as he held her. One doctor came out and said that they were not sure if she would make it through the day, but they had to wait and see, and the senior doctor would come out to talk with them. (This was Will's first wife, Ruth Ann Richardson).

"Ava, go call the others while I wait for the other doctor."

When Ava left, Will was really upset (not showing his emotions outwardly). He was hoping that Ava's mother would be OK and, on the other hand, praying that Isabella's mother didn't find out about Ava's mother.

When Ava returned, Will had been in to see her mother. He prayed with her and told her she was pretty banged up, but she would be all right. He told Ava that he needed to go get something to drink and walk for a moment and that he had some business to tend to. He told her the doctor said that her mother would make it, but it's going to take some time. He also told Ava to go refresh herself in the bathroom and go get something to eat. He would be back to check on her and her mom. This was his excuse to leave and go check on Isabella's mother.

When Will came back to Ruth Ann's room, she had had the baby, and it was a little girl. When he saw the child and Ruth Ann, he could not stop kissing both of them. Ruth Ann was looking so beautiful, and the baby was too. All of a sudden, Will looked at me and said, "Ruth Ann, please never leave me." I said, "OK," then he said, "Promise me before God that you will never leave me."

I said, "OK. Are you OK?"

He said, "Yes. Just the thought of not being with you would kill me."

I said, "Now, Will. What, man, in the world would take me and two brats?"

We both started to laugh. "Ann, I love you so much, and I want to give you everything."

I told Will, "All right. I am not dying or anything. I am going home in the next few days."

"Ann, you just look beautiful."

I just looked and smiled for a moment. "Even with my hair like this?"

"Yes, even so."

She said, "OK. Let's name the baby Samantha."

Will said, "Samam what?"

I told him, "Don't worry," that he would learn how to pronounce the baby's name before she got eighteen. (Both of us were laughing). Will told me that he had to leave and call Cousin Sylvia and get things ready for our coming home.

When Will left Ruth Ann's room (Samantha's mother) he went back downstairs to the waiting room with Ava. When Ava saw her dad (Will), she asked him where he went. He told her to clear his head for a moment. "Ava asked him has the doctor come out to talk to you anymore?" He told her yes. He said, "It's going to be a long recovery time."

About that time, the other children had arrived. They all went in to see their mother. Will told them to go ahead. He had to make some calls, and he would be in there in a minute.

Dad called Cousin Sylvia and told her the good news that Ann and the baby (Samantha) were both fine and resting. He described me as a beautiful, dark-skinned little girl with silky black hair with a touch of light red or brown. He told her that I looked like his mother. Then Will asked whether Big Lue, Cousin Sylvia's husband, was home.

She said, "Hold for a moment."

Big Lue came on the phone laughing, telling Will he heard Ruth Ann and Cousin Sylvia talking about how he reacted when Ruth Ann said it was time to have the baby by jumping straight up. (They were both laughing.)

THAT NIGHT, WILL did not go home. He went to the house of the other Ruth Ann (his first wife), who was in the accident, as all his other children were meeting there. In the next few days, Will would visit Samantha's mom and Ava's mother at the hospital too. Will realized that he was going to have to tell Ava and the other children about his new wife and family. Will was not sure how to or when to tell Isabella and Samantha's mom. The thought of him telling her was breaking his heart; he even had tears running down his face because he knew that she was going to take it badly with all she had been through. He hated that he did not tell her about being married before and about the children. The weight of this situation was weighing heavily on his shoulders, as he could not bring himself to tell her.

Cousin Sylvia called the hospital and inquired about Ruth Ann. The receptionist asked for the middle name because there was more than one person in the hospital with the same name. Cousin Sylvia said, "Now ain't that something. Wow, you are kidding me." She shook it off and gave the receptionist Ruth Ann's middle name. When Cousin Sylvia and Big Lue arrived at the hospital with Isabella, Daddy was already there. Everyone was so excited about the new arrival, Samantha. Ruth Ann stayed in the hospital for about five days, and then she was released from the hospital. By that time, Will had told Ava and the other children about his marriage and the two children Isabella and Samantha. Ava was not really upset because Daddy and her mother were already separated, and they were all grown up, so they figured he would find someone else. Yet he occasionally came to their house and visited.

Samantha's Story

When we arrived home, Daddy, had made a little rocking bed for me. Mommy was really surprised and happy. At that moment, Mommy was really happy. She said that all of her dreams were coming true. She screamed out, "THANK YOU, LORD."

Later that night, Daddy asked Mommy if he could go walking to get a little fresh air. Mommy said, "Sure, Will. Don't be out long." Daddy would go to the phone booth at the corner store to call and check on my other sisters and brothers. Nate, William, James, Ava, Michelle, and Rebecca and their mother, always returning home within forty-five minutes to an hour. Isabella and Samantha's mother was brought up in a time when a girl's light complexion or whiteness would get you somewhere in life, but if you were of darker skin, society only allowed you to wash clothes for the white people or light-skinned people. You were treated as a lower class of people. So, mentally, she had a hard time with the color of my skin. Even though she loved me, she did not like my color. Mommy had seen how society would treat the darker-colored girls, and she was upset that she thought people would treat me badly. It was not just the white folks, but even our own race would treat darker-skinned girls differently. Now if you were a dark-skinned boy, you were OK because you could do those hard jobs, and yes, you were a boy.

11

MY PARENTS ENJOYED taking long walks in the evening and early on Saturday mornings. Mommy would never push us. She always told Daddy to push those different-colored children. Daddy would shake his head and push us. As we became older, Mommy loved to dress up Isabella and I. She always brought us beautiful dresses and laced socks. We never wore cheap shoes as Mommy would often say, "Buster Brown shoes are the best for kids." Mommy enjoyed fixing our hair with ribbons to match whatever we were going to wear that day. Wow, could she fix herself up as well. Everyone in the neighborhood would say, "Classy diva." Daddy's friends would always say, "Will, man, you got you a good-looking woman there." Daddy would say, "And remember she is all mine," with a smile.

Our home was always neat and clean. Mommy would often look at magazines for new ideas to improve our home. Everything was always in place. If you moved anything, she knew it. Cooking breakfast and dinner or any meal was always enjoyable. When Daddy would go to work, he had enough lunch to share with his coworkers. Sometimes, they would make special requests and would pay for the meals. She could bake like no other, making everything from scratch. She would often say, "God showed me how to do these things, and if we would listen to God, he would show us how to do what he created you to do to share with others." Our birthdays were very memorable and fun. Daddy often would pick us up and twirl us around. When Daddy would come home from work, we would run to the door to greet him every day (as if we had not seen him for days).

I remember this one time, Mommy took us over at Cousin Sylvia's house to play with our cousins, little Lue and Frances. While we were playing in the room, all of a sudden, we heard a lot of yelling and arguing. We could not tell what it was all about, but soon, Mommy came inside the room where Isabella and I were. She was really mad and said, "We are going home right *now*!" She was upset. We had never seen her so mad that it scared us, so we did not say anything all the way home. When we arrived at home, Mommy seemed a little calmer; she fixed dinner, gave us our bath (always humming or singing spiritual songs while bathing us), read the Bible to us, and we went to sleep. If Daddy was not there when we ate dinner, she often left his plate in the oven. That night, Isabella and I woke up when we heard our parents yelling (mainly Mommy). Daddy kept saying, "Now, Ann. Calm down. If I did not love you, I would not be here."

Mommy said, "But you were married and have children," and asking him, "When did you get a divorce?"

Daddy paused and said, "I did not have to."

Mommy really did yell then. "WHAT?"

Daddy said, "Now, Ruth Ann, because I had not been with her for years. The law says I am divorced."

Mommy said, "Well, you had better be sure of that, Will."

Mommy said, "Now do you have any more secrets up your sleeves that I should know about?"

"No. Ruth Ann, I love you and want to spend all of my life with you and our children only."

Mommy said, "Now, Will, how many other children do you have?"

Daddy said, "Five more."

"I cannot believe it. Five more children. OK, what are their names and ages? And none better not be around Samantha's age."

Daddy said, "Of course not. Nate is the oldest, William—they call him Lil Will—James, Ava, Michelle, and Rebecca. They are all grown and the oldest is about a few years older than you, and the youngest is about a couple of years younger than you."

"OK. What is their mother's name?"

Daddy paused for a moment and said, "Well, her name is Ruth Ann."

Mommy said a lot of bad words (damn). "XXO, what were you thinking? What the XXO." Mommy went into the room, got Daddy's cover and pillow, and threw it at him. Mommy said, "Now I know what you mean that you are the luckiest man in this here world!" while yelling excessively. She walked back into her room, saying, "Lord, please forgive me. Please forgive me."

The next morning, all I remember is Isabella and I playing with our toys until dinner time. It was different this time, being so quiet. But I just could not stop talking, telling Daddy the things we had done and learned. I said we played doll babies and we went over to Cousin Sylvia's house, but then Mommy and Cousin Sylvia were arguing, and Mommy left mad. Mommy said, "Hush up, Samantha, and eat."

Isabella said, "After we eat, can you tell us a story?"

Mommy said, "Now, Isabella, you hush up too. You all just eat your food."

Daddy said he would tell us a story before we went to bed. Mommy said, "He is good at making up lies, oh, I mean stories."

Daddy never replied to what Mommy had said. He just looked at her and then kept on eating. That night, Daddy told us a story about two beautiful little girls and their beautiful mother. How they lived in a big house with a white picket fence, and they had a dog. Isabella said, "Can I name the dog, Daddy?"

Daddy said, "Sure, little darling."

Isabella said, "The dog's name is Rover." We all laughed.

In the story, each of us had our own room with all of our favorite toys. Then he said, "It's getting late now. We will finish the story tomorrow because we have to go to church in the morning."

The next morning it was church time. We loved going to church; the people would get happy, dancing and singing. The preacher would tell us some good lessons on living. That day, Daddy and Mommy were really quiet. After church, we went home. Isabella and I always enjoyed playing together. The next few weeks at home were noticeably quiet. Before that day, wow, I remember during Christmas and the holidays, Mommy always made it exciting. Mommy would decorate the apartment so beautifully and cook a lot of cakes, pies, and candies to sell to the neighbors. We would watch Mommy make the cakes and pies and could hardly wait to get the scraps of the yummy bowl of cake mix to eat. She would help us make our own cake or pie. Daddy's tradition was for us to decorate a box, and on Christmas Day, we would find lots and lots of candies, apples, oranges, nuts, and money along with a letter from Santa Claus, stating we had been really good children. When Daddy would watch baseball, always sitting in his favorite chair (recliner), he often would fall asleep, and when a player would hit a home run or something exciting would happen and the crowd would show excitement, Daddy would wake up shouting and saying, "What happened?" several times. Mommy would say, "One day, you are going to watch all of that game that you like so much" while laughing a little.

12

ONE DAY, AT home, Daddy and Mommy were playing jacks with us, and someone knocked on the door. Daddy said, "I'll get the door, Ann."

It was a bunch of people, and they were yelling at Daddy. Daddy said, "You bring this to my home with my family? Let's take this outside."

Mommy said for us to stay in the house as she went outside with Daddy too. We could not hear what was going on, but we could see a lot of people outside. Isabella and I tried to lift the window up, so we could hear. As we lift the window up and began listening, all of a sudden, the window came falling down, and my pinky was stuck. I was screaming and crying. Isabella tried to get the window up but could not, so she ran outside to tell our parents. They both came running inside. Daddy lifted the window off my finger, and Mommy grabbed me. "It is your fault, Will. Look at Samantha's finger."

He did not say a word and just looked at my finger. They checked to see if I needed to go to the hospital, but I did not. The finger was squished and bruised, not broken. I cannot remember what happened after that day whether my parents went back outside or not, but I do remember them telling us, "It's going to be OK, children," as Isabella and I were both crying. This was the turning point of my mother's dreams being shattered. She told Daddy that she tried but could no longer trust him after finding out he was still married to the other Ruth Ann. Daddy pleaded with her, but she was so hurt that she could not trust anything he would say anymore. "This is too, too much confusion, and I don't want our children exposed to arguments and fighting." She told him she needed some time.

Daddy yelled, "Saying time for *what*? I am here with you, and I love you and our children."

"So now I should believe what you say?"

He explained that he did not know he was not divorced if they did not live together. Mommy said, "Will, you assured me you would get that straight. Now our marriage is not legal, and I have two bastard children."

Daddy did not say anything for a moment, then he dropped to his knees and said, "But, Ann, I really do love you," with tears running down his face. "I am so sorry. Please, Ann."

Mommy said, "No, Will. Not this time. You have had every opportunity to get this mess straight, but you just ignore it as if it's going to go away on its own."

O.L. HARRISON

13

WELL, IT SEEMED like the pages of life were going at an accelerated pace. Soon, Will started staying out really late and not coming straight home from work. When he did arrive at home, you could smell the liquor as if he had taken a bath in it. One night, Ruth Ann said, "I am going to kill that no-good Will. I know he is going out on me with other ladies," while talking on the phone to Cousin Sylvia.

That evening, Ruth Ann fixed dinner as usual. She bathed us, read a story to us, and prayed with us. She often told us the Bible stories about Jonah and the whale, Queen Esther, David and the lion's den. After she prayed with us, she told us, "Now, girls, stay in the room and go to sleep. Don't get out of the bed even if you hear a lot of noise."

Isabella said, "What kind of noise, Mommy?"

Ruth Ann replied, "Well if you hear me yelling at your daddy."

Samantha asked, "Why are you going to yell at Daddy?"

Ruth Ann replied, "It is grownup stuff. Now hush now and go to sleep." Ruth Ann walked out of the room, telling the girls, "Sweet dreams."

That night Isabella and Samantha could not go to sleep. They went to the bedroom door and peeped out. Ruth Ann was sitting in front of the door with the shotgun. Isabella said, "Ooooh wee, Mommy's going to kill Daddy tonight." Samantha asked Isabella why. Isabella told her that she did not know, but it must be grownup stuff.

We fell asleep at the bedroom door. We heard Daddy coming up the stairs, singing, as he often did; we ran out of the room and yelled, "Daddy, don't come in. Mommy got the shotgun!"

Mommy must have fallen asleep because she jumped and the shotgun went off. We heard someone running down the stairs. Our mom was really mad at us. She said, "Did not I tell you two to not get out of the bed?"

We began to cry. Mommy put us back to bed, and she went to sleep beside us while humming softly). Daddy did not come back home that night. But on Sunday morning, he returned home. Mommy told Daddy, "Your mixed-up children saved your black behind this time."

Will said, "Ruth Ann, are you going crazy? You're going to kill a man for drinking a little?"

Ruth Ann said, "Yes, I sure am 'cause I ain't no fool."

Will got dressed and we all went to church. He knew that Sundays was the Lord's day, so Ruth Ann would not really argue or make a big fuss on the Lord's day. Will tried, or attempted to try, to make the marriage work, talking to Ruth Ann excessively. He told her, "Let me take my only true love out on a date. Please, Ann, please. Let's start over, Ann."

Ruth Ann would look at him and ignore him, but after a couple of weeks, she finally gave in and said, "OK, Will."

So that Friday night, they took Isabella and Samantha to Ruth Ann's Cousin Sylvia's house, and off they went to the bar. Ruth Ann was attractive and could really dance, so men would ask if she would want to dance, and she would say to Will, "Do you mind?" And he said, "Of course not. Go ahead have fun."

Every time they would go out on the weekends, Will would be mad when he came back home. telling Ruth Ann, "I said you could dance with other men, not letting them get that close to you."

Ruth Ann said, "OK. I was just punishing you a little. I won't do that anymore."

One weekend after they had talked, Will's daughter, Ava, was at the bar, and she came over and asked Will to dance while Ruth Ann was on the dance floor. Ruth Ann saw him dancing, so she did it again, letting the man she was dancing with get too close to her. But this time, Will told his daughter, "Excuse me for a minute," and he went over and cut in on Ruth Ann and the man's dance. He whispered in her ear, "I thought we talked about you not letting men get too close to you?"

Ruth Ann whispered back, "We did, but when I say you dancing with that woman, I got a little jealous."

Will told her, "Well, Ann, that was my oldest daughter."

O.L. HARRISON

Ann replied, "Oh, and that man was my oldest son."

Laughing, Will said, "No, really, Ann.

Ann said, "OK. I still have some trust issues, Will." After looking closer at the woman, she realized it was his daughter.

14

The Move to Brooklyn

TRYING TO PUT some distance between the two families our parents decided to move. Wilkinson Avenue on the third floor in Brooklyn, New York; it was exciting. We had to pack up many boxes. Ruth Ann told her sisters the move was best for the family. Putting a little distance between some things. (The grownups knew what she meant.) Things were really nice at the new place for a while until Mommy received a call from someone, and the next thing Isabella and Samantha knew was that their mother said they were going to play a game and get rid of Daddy's old clothes.

Ruth Ann told the girls to go to the window, and when they saw their daddy reach the tree, they were going to call him and throw those old clothes away because it is easier for him to get instead of coming all the way upstairs and then take them downstairs.

The kids were excited about learning a new game. (Will had been with another woman, and Ruth Ann was fed up with his lies). Samantha had to stand at the window as Isabella and her mother went to get her dad's stuff. Isabella asked her mother if her dad was going to be mad because the stuff was some of his good stuff. Ruth Ann said, "No. He is going to buy some better stuff."

Isabella was excited. We waited a long time, but when he finally came, we began to throw his stuff out the window, saying, "Look, Daddy. Catch." Ruth Ann looked like she was trying to hit Will with his shoes. Will did not go upstairs that day; he just picked up what he could and left. Samantha yelled, "Daddy, where are you going?"

He yelled and said, "I will be back later, little darling."

Later that night, Will called Ruth Ann to come back home, but Ruth Ann told him that she could not stay with her anymore as not only was he cheating with another woman, but he had not straightened out the situation about their marriage. She told Will she loved him, but she loved herself more, and that she did not believe God wanted her to be a fool. She also told him that she had her girls to think about and would not want them to grow up to be a fool either. She told him that she was an example for her children and of the teachings of her parents. Will told her Ruth Ann, "You are the only woman I ever absolutely loved. You pushed me into another woman's bed because you would not allow me to make love with you. But you are the one and only woman I *love*."

Ruth Ann told Will, "Yeah right. You pushed yourself 'cause you lied and lied and lied and kept staying out late, not me. You, Will. That is just an excuse for you to do what you want to do."

Will pleaded with Ruth Ann but she stood firm. "No is *no*. Not this time. I deserve better than this." Ruth Ann said bye to Will.

Will was still talking, saying, "Wait, Ann. When am I going to see the children?"

"When you get a place, you can get them on the weekends."

"What? Just the weekends? If you want to come get them during the week after school, you can." Will paused in silence for a moment as Ruth Ann stated, "Will, are you there?"

Will said, "Yes, I am here." Will said, "OK, Ann. I will talk to you tomorrow if that is OK?" Ruth Ann said it's ok. Will told her if she needed anything to let him know.

She said, "OK, Will. Bye," before hanging up the phone. Even though Ruth Ann never let anyone see her cry or upset, the children saw their mother's countenance seem extremely sad.

WILL CALLED RUTH Ann and talked with the children every day. Most of the time, two to three times during the day. At night, Will would call and tell Ruth Ann how much he missed her and the children, asking to come home with the answer always being *no*. We would see Daddy at church, but he would not come home with us. The children missed him a lot and did not understand why he was not at home. Ruth Ann would often tell the children to "be big girls 'cause your dad is working away and will not be coming home. He will pick you girls up on the weekends and call you a lot."

Samantha remembered her dad telling Isabella and herself that they had other sisters and brothers, naming them Nate, William (Little Will), James, Ava, Michelle, and Rebecca. Wow, did Isabella and Samantha ask him a lot of questions, When can we see them?" "How old are they?" "Where are they?" "What's their mother's name?"

Will just said, "Now hold on here. Never mind the questions. I just wanted you to know."

(Samantha telling the story) I don't remember meeting all of them altogether, but I remember meeting Ava and Little Will at Daddy's place. As months passed, Daddy did not call us every day anymore but maybe once or twice a week, and then we stopped going to visit Daddy every weekend but maybe once or twice a week a month. Isabella and I enjoyed watching cartoons with Daddy, laughing and coloring, walks in the park, and we loved to swing. We had to read, he would tell Isabella and me to write out addition, subtraction, and multiplication. We could hardly wait to finish the work to get some ice cream and a piece of candy.

16

A COUPLE OF years had passed since my parents were separated. When we would go to the grocery store, this man was always following us around saying hi to our mother. One day, he finally asked Mommy for her name and introduced himself as Harold. He was the assistant manager at the grocery store. He asked Mommy if she would like to go out to dinner and a movie this weekend? She said sure. Then they exchanged information and time. He came over often always bringing Isabella and me some candy. Then Mommy would put us in the bed, and we would pretend that we were asleep. They would be laughing and listening to soft music. One night, I (Samantha) got out of bed to go to the bathroom, and I saw Mommy kissing Mr. Harold. I just stood there, and when Mommy saw me, she jumped up and came over and spanked me. While spanking me, she said, "Didn't I tell you to go to bed?" I was trying to tell Mommy I had to go to the bathroom. I wet myself while she was spanking me all over the floor. Mommy told Mr. Harold, "Sorry. Another time."

He tried to convince her to just put me back to bed, but Mommy said, "No, sorry. You are going to have to leave now." So he left. She washed me up and changed my clothes and put me back to bed. Isabella was acting like she was asleep. I was still weeping, so she said, "Now hush. Just go to sleep. You were just dreaming."

When Mommy left the room, Isabella came over and asked me was I ok and what happened? I told her that I saw Mr. Harold kissing Mommy and touching her. Isabella said, "Aw, I guess that's what grown folks do." She allowed me to get in her bed and rocked me until we both fell asleep.

THINGS HAD CHANGED tremendously. Mommy did not sing as much anymore, just occasionally. We went to visit Daddy at his job, as Daddy and Mommy talked, he told Mommy that if anything was to happen to him, he had an insurance policy for her and us, so we could go to college. He also told Mommy that he had a life too, and if she did not want him, well, he had to live. Mommy said, "Well, that's true. After they finished talking, he brought us into the warehouse where he stored the books and music boxes. He showed us the machines and talked to us about going to college. He said, "Be sure you be a secretary or work in an office." He told us that, one day, he would die, and he wanted us to know that he loved our mother and us very much.

We asked Daddy, "Why people have to die?"

He said, "The same reason why people have to be born. That is how God planned it. We come from him to make a choice. We go back to him at the end of our choice. It's God's way of giving us a new body, like a pair of shoes when they wear out, you get another pair. Same with us when our old body wears out, we get a new one."

When Daddy talked, we always listened. The only thing that did not change was the way Mommy carried herself, and her appearance was always nice (ours too). Mommy was determined that her children and herself would always have the best. Mommy would often tell us that "people are not going to give you anything. You have to go and get what you want. And no matter the circumstance that comes into your life, remember there is a God who will always take care of you. Ask God daily for forgiveness and forgive others. Remember the Ten Commandments: 'Thou shalt have no other gods before me, Thou shalt not worship any graven image, Thou shalt not take God's name in vain, Remember the Sabbath to keep it holy, Honor thy father and thy mother, Thou shalt not kill, Thou shalt not commit adultery, Thou shalt not steal, Thou shalt not bear false witness, Thou shalt not covet; Always remember trust in the Lord with your whole heart and lean not to your own understanding in all your ways acknowledge the Lord and he will direct your path. And always go to church.'"

AS YEARS PASSED, I remember one night in part when Mommy had gone to the bar with some friends. Upon her return, we could hear other people in the house saying, "She is going to be OK. Just let her sleep it off."

She said, "No. Call my brother," as she was acting strange. Uncle Liam came to take her to the hospital. The doctors said someone had spiked her drink and, they would have to keep her in the hospital for a while to figure out what it was and how to treat her. At first, Isabella and I stayed with Cousin Sylvia and her family. They took us to see Mommy while she was in the hospital. The hospital had bars on the windows. It really looked scary. After a couple of months, Mommy came home. Mommy did really well for a long time, then she would start acting strange again. Whatever someone spiked her drink with affected her ability to think rationally. It seemed that, at times, she would be thinking normally, but then her thoughts would get scrambled up, not thinking normally anymore. When her thoughts were off, she would throw out all of our furniture, clothes, shoes, TVs, coats, underwear, and so much more. People would go to the dumpster and pick up the stuff as if they were at Macy's department store or something. Mommy always brought nice stuff and kept it as if it was new. Then Mommy would go back into the hospital, but soon, Cousin Sylvia could not keep us. Uncle Lue was sick. When we were with Cousin Sylvia, we could still go see our dad. Cousin Sylvia told us she loved us, but that Uncle Lue was really sick and that Uncle Liam was coming to get us until Mommy came home.

When Uncle Liam arrived, we were ready. He explained that we were going to his house, but that he had to leave and go to work, so we would be with our aunt Abigail and our other cousins. Wow, on the surface we thought all was well. But when he left, we soon found out that we were in hell. Aunt Abigail would often tell us that our mother thought "she was all that. Now, look at her." (We later found out that the married man that our mother had had Isabella by was Aunt Abigail's sister's husband, Paul.) We did not find this information out until we were adults ourselves. Aunt Abigail a beautician, was a quiet drunk with lots of issues. I now believed she did the best for all of us. She had eight children: Alicia, Diane, Raymond (Lil Ray), Barbara Sue, Ted Calvin, and Scott; and her three nephews, Sam, Robert, and Craig; and now Isabella and me (Samantha). She would take our clothes and put it on her girls, making sure they looked good too. When she would fix our hair, she would say, "Tie your hair up every night before you go to sleep," and that we need to learn to share because we did not like taking our clothes and giving to our cousins.

She worked from her home. If any of her clients did not hold their ears, well, many have gotten, burned several times. She also sewed. Sometimes our cousins and us would argue. We said they were ugly, and they said, "So your mother is crazy." Then we would fight. Our aunt Abigail would tell us every day that the only reason why our mother would act crazy like that was because she did not want us. (She did not understand our mother was sick and what had happened to her).

During bath time, my aunt would come in the bathroom and say, "Damn, Samantha you are black as tar" while pouring some bleach in the water. She would say, "Soak in this for a while. Maybe you will get lighter." While all of this was going on, my mother was in the hospital, and my uncle Liam did not know. I remember one of my cousins. That boy would make me go into the room with him while he would rub on my private parts and lie on me. My aunt was so drunk, she never knew what was going on in the house. I remember always being scared, and Isabella would say to stay close to her because she could fight.

For the most part, we played nicely together, but there were times when they would tell us that we thought we were better than they were and saying, "Yeah right. That's why you are with us because you are better" while laughing. Isabella and I did act like we thought we were better, but we just wanted to be better. I cannot remember what happened this one time we were arguing, and they kicked us out of the living room where everyone gathered to play pool and watch TV.(more like a game room). We kept on pleading to let us come back in to play and watch TV. One of our cousins said, "Let's let them in," as they were tired of us nagging them. They grabbed Isabella and held her down as she was kicking and fighting them back, and they were painting her face red with lipstick. Isabella yelled to me and said, "Hide, Samantha. Hide." Then one of the other cousins grabbed a rat trap with a dead mouse on it, and all the children went running. We ran into the room and got under the cover as he ran the rat across us as we were screaming. They stopped when my aunt woke up and said, "Stop all that damn noise now!"

When my aunt Abigail would fix dinner. Her children and the nephews would eat first, and whatever was left we would eat. Rarely did we all eat together, only, when Uncle Liam was there at dinner time. I remember I was so hungry one Saturday morning, and everyone was looking for me. Ha, ha. I was in the pantry where they kept the flour. I had gotten a cup of water and got in the pantry, eating flour and drinking water. When my aunt found me, she said, "Now, ain't this some shit. This little black boot gone in the flour bin" as she was laughing. She was saying like "a little white sandboy." Another time, I remember drinking some water and I had not noticed a roach was in the cup until it almost was at my lips. Boy, was I spitting every where. Isabella laughed and laughed, saying, "What's wrong, Samantha? You did not want any caviar with your water?"

When Mommy would get well, we would go back home. It was like moving to a new home because we had to buy new furniture and things.

19

WE LIVED IN a low-income housing, better known as the project. Mommy made sure that even though we lived in the projects, we did not have to look or act like we were less than anyone else. She taught us that our appearance showed how we felt about ourselves, and people look at that first, then they listen to you, and third people, watch how you act. If you master these three things, people will always treat you right, at least most of the time. God will see to it if you do your part. Do all your work in school and be respectful. A person of integrity never gets in with the wrong people. Isabella and I said, "Yes, Ma." Every night, Mommy would read the Bible to us. The stories about Jonah and the whale, David and Goliath, Samson, Queen Esther, Adam and Eve, Samuel the prophet, and Abraham and Sarah. Things would be wonderful with Mommy, but she would get sick, and back to Aunt Abigail's house we would be. This happened so many times that I cannot remember. Aunt Abigail always reminded Isabella and me that Mommy really did not want us and that Mommy was just pretending to get away from us. This was due to our aunt's lack of understanding of our mother's illness. We began to dislike Mommy because we had heard so many bad things about her from our aunt that, one time, when Mommy came back from the hospital, we said, "What do you want?" And Mommy just looked and she said, "Come here."

Isabella said, "For what?" And I said, "Yeah, for what?"

She came over, grabbed Isabella and me, and she took us in the room and did we get a fanning that would last us for the rest of our lives. From that day until this day, I remember never to disrespect my mother. A lesson well learned. She told us that she whipped us because she loved us, and we were never to act like that again. We said, "Yes, Ma." Isabella said she was sorry, and I, Samantha, said I was sorry too.

There was an occasion when Mommy got sick, and she was really in a bad way. She would not let us out of her bedroom. We had to stay in the bed with her while she was on her cycle. Blood was on us, and the smell was disgusting. Mommy's eyes looked like they were popping out of her head, and she would make very strange noises at times, sounding like a frog. We were so scared of her, making us throw away things. She seemed really scary, saying she had to protect us. We stayed in the room with no water or food, TV, radio, or telephone. The impact of that day left us traumatized to the degree that I can only remember bits and pieces of how we got out of that room. I remember images of a firefighter, my uncle Liam, the police, and an ambulance. I cannot remember if they took us to the hospital or even if we had to stay in the hospital. All I remember was that we were back at Aunt Abigail's house again. That time glad to be there. That time was different from all the other times. Before, when we went to Aunt Abigail's house, we would have to catch the train to go from her house in Harlem to Jamaica Queens to get to school. When Isabella and I were on the train on our way to school, we fell to sleep and missed our stop. We had missed most of school, so we just waited at the subway until it was time to go back to Aunt Abigail's house again. We tried not to fall to sleep anymore as we were really scared before. God sent us an angel in the form of a little old lady. That angel would make sure, when our stop was coming up, that she would tell us, so we would not miss it.

My aunt Abigail had to enroll us in a school in her neighborhood. After a couple of months of us being at the new school, my uncle Pete and aunt Sophia came up from Southern Pines to visit Mommy and to check on us. While our aunt Sophia and uncle Pete were there, Aunt Abigail made sure she treated us right. Uncle Liam came home too. He did this trick where he could take us with one foot and hold us upside down with one hand. Everyone was always amazed when he would do that trick.

We all went to see Mommy at the hospital. When Mommy saw us, she picked us up and kissed us. We sat in her lap as she recited the Lord's Prayer with her, "Our Father who art in heaven, hallowed be thy name. Thy kingdom come. Thy will be done on earth as it is in heaven. Give us this day our daily bread and forgive us our trespasses, as we forgive those who trespass against us, and lead us not into temptation but deliver us from evil. For thine is the power and the glory forevermore. Amen." Then we would hug some more. She talked with her sister and brother then we left.

Our uncle Liam told us we might be moving out of town when our mother comes home. He said we might spend the summer with our cousins in Southern Pines, North Carolina. My aunt Sophia sent her daughter, Mary Ann, up to Manhattan to help Aunt Abigail out.

20

ISABELLA AND I just loved Sundays because, every Sunday Aunt, Abigail would send all the children to church, saying she needed a break. I wish I could recall the church's name because the word of God says "to render therefore to all their . . . honor to who honor is due" (Rom. 13:7). At church, the service was always wonderful, and the choir would sing the most beautiful songs you would ever hear. The preacher would always preach a word from the Bible that would encourage our hearts to want more of the word of God. Wow, could those women cook! After church, we would eat the best food ever. The chicken was fried exactly right, crispy and tender inside and seasoned perfectly. I enjoyed every bite. The collard greens, potato salad, macaroni and cheese, rice, and the string beans were simply delicious. They had made every kind of dessert we could think about—peach cobbler, apple cobbler, coconut pie, sweet potato pie, chocolate cake, yellow cake, German chocolate cake, and banana pudding, just to name a few. If you were not drawn in by the word of God, you sure would be drawn in by the people's love, food, and hospitality. They always welcomed us and made us feel like we belonged. Their demonstration of love was shown in how they served others. They also had a clothing closet that they would announce. If anyone needed any clothing, they had some new items available. They offered to tutor anyone who needed assistance in school or reading. I cannot remember running into anyone person at that church who made me feel like I did not belong. Because of their demonstration of love, the seed they planted did not fall on hard ground but began to grow in us. Isn't that what the church is supposed to do? That church lady, Elder Elaine, would make sure that each of us had some food to take home and some clothes. They never looked for anything in return because their kindness and genuine love kept us coming. We joined the children's chore and sometimes they let us stand at the door to greet people coming in with the older ushers. This really did build our self-esteem. Because most people related us as the children with the crazy mother. That act of kindness from God's house was engraved in our hearts. People would sometimes say "there is a call on these children".

During summers, we would go swimming and to the library. I remember this one time when we went to the pool, a girl that came with us, had put on her bathing suit. She did not have any boobs yet, so she would stuff her top with stockings. Some boy pushed her in the water. When she came up, the stockings came out floating. Boy, oh, boy, did we laugh. She grabbed those stockings and ran to the locker room to fix It and came back in the pool like nothing had happened. That made it even funnier.

Aunt Abigail struggled to provide for all of us. When I was younger, I thought my aunt Abigail was mean, but I could see now that she was trying her best because it could have been worst for us. I cannot imagine struggling with my children and eleven more children. I am hopeful I would do better, but who knows. I believe that if someone had taken the time to explain things to us, we would have been better. All of the things that happened in our lives did not make us bitter but made us better. Aunt Abigail was fighting with her own demons, not allowing herself to get free, drowning in her own sorrow and pain.

My mother was struggling with the acceptance that she had to now take all of that medicine to stay well and not understand why.

21

MOMMY WAS STABLE for about two or three years. We were able to reconnect with Daddy, seeing him on weekends more regularly and hearing from him again. Life was normal for us again. About a year later, Mommy called Daddy as usual to let him know we needed some shoes, but she could not reach him. She called various times to no avail, even calling his job. Joe, at his job, stated that he had been out for a couple of weeks. Mommy had asked Cousin Sylvia to check with Big Lue to see if he had heard from him, but Big Lue was so sick and Cousin Sylvia said that Will hadn't called their house in a while. Mommy decided to go over to Daddy's apartment to check on him.

Mommy made the trip to Daddy's apartment fun with us singing and playing punch cars, spelling words we saw, and color games she made up. When we arrived at Daddy's apartment, we knocked and knocked, but no one came to the door. Then we started yelling for him, and finally, a man came to the door and said, "What is all the ruckus about?"

Mommy told him she was looking for William Richardson. (This was a rooming house.) As Mommy described him, he told her that he had moved and did not know where he moved to. Mommy said, "What?" Mommy turned red as a bird and said, "Come on. To hell with him." On the way back, she had calmed down, saying, "It is not like your dad. I hope he is OK."

Mommy kept trying to find Daddy. She even called the landlord of the place he was last staying at, but they said he had paid up his rent and moved without any forwarding address. She went to his job and stayed from the time he would go to work until the time he would normally leave, but still no Daddy. She checked with the police department, but still, they could not find Daddy. She called Cousin Sylvia and said, "Will would never just abandon us like that. Something is wrong."

Cousin Sylvia said that she had been so busy taking care of Big Lue that she had not had a chance to check around, but she would and would let her know as soon as she heard anything. Later, the next day, Cousin Sylvia called Mommy to tell her she had checked with some of their friends, and no one has heard from him, but as soon as she could find out, she would let her know.

Mommy told us that Daddy had gone on a business trip, and he would call us later. When she would put us to bed, we would imagine all the wonderful places that Daddy could be and that he would soon come and get us to show us all the wonderful places that were in the world. Years had passed, and we had not heard from our dad, but Mom would make up stuff like he had called while we were sleep or school. She was always saying he loved us so much and that we were going to be a family again and live in a big house with each of us having our own room. We were always happy. In Dads' absence Mommy realized she really did want the family back together.

22

FOR THE LONGEST time, Mommy was mentally stable, and everything was good. We were experiencing normal life. Mommy always read books to us, and we played the game called trouble practically every night. Isabella and I loved to color in our coloring book and play with papier-mâché.

During the summer, we had a ball. The adults would get together and turn the fire hydrant on for fun, and we would enjoy playing in the water, playing double Dutch, and playing skelly. Skelly is an outdoor game that we played on the ground with jar tops and bottle tops. In our neighborhood, we were like a big family. We later moved again, and I cannot recall the place we moved to, but it was in Brooklyn. That neighborhood was like family also except there was a church bus that would come and pick up people to go to church. We would all meet to get on the bus on Sunday mornings, and after church, the bus driver would take us to the movies, bowling, to the park, and once a month, for a big outing. The two best places I remember going to was to the zoo and Hershey Park. Most of the parents did not go to church, but Mommy always went with us.

In the evening time, the parents would get the trash can and stuff paper into it and light it as they sat on the benches and talked about their day and the latest gossip while the children would play. We were never allowed to fight each other as, no matter what, both children would get discipline (spanking). So there were few problems among the children.

Going to school was fun. One of the neighbors had a berry tree, and she allowed us to pick the tree for our snacks. At school, the girls had to go in the door for girls, and the boys had to go in the door for boys. The boys and girls were not in the same classrooms either.

Mommy had stopped taking her medicine as someone told her she needed to have faith, and yes, she was sick again. This time, she did not stay sick exceedingly long (about two weeks). We were back at Aunt Abigail's house again, but this time, we knew the drill, and we did not have to take all of our clothes and stuff over to her house. When Mommy came out of the hospital this time, Aunt Abigail told her, "Ruth Ann girl, you need a man. You need to go out and enjoy yourself."

Mommy told her, "Yeah, girl, you are right. I am going to go get me a turkey tonight." And she did. She went to the bar and met a man named Mason. We saw him a lot for a while, then Mommy told us she was pregnant, and we were going to have a brother or sister. It was fun touching Mommy's stomach while the baby was kicking and moving around inside her. After the baby was born, Mommy gave him his father's first and middle name and our last name, Mason W. He was adorable, always smiling. His nickname was Little Mason.

Mason was about seven months old when our mother became sick again. And yes, we were back at Aunt Abigail's house. Wow, did Aunt Abigail fuss and cuss this time because now she had a baby to take care of along with her eight children, three nephews, and us three, a total of twelve children. Some were teenagers.

When Uncle Liam came to check on us, he told Aunt Abigail, "Damn, Abigail comb that boy's head or something," left her some money, and left. So my Aunt Abigail took Lil Mason into the kitchen and shaved his head. We all were scared and speechless as we heard Mason crying in the kitchen. We stood by the door, listening. My cousin said, "I think she is giving him a haircut."

My mother always liked Lil Mason's hair as she would say, "Look at my little African king." So Isabella said, "Boy, oh, boy. Mommy is going to be mad, mad, mad."

When she came out of the kitchen with Lil Mason, he looked scared, and she gave him to Isabella. Isabella held him, and we played with him until he went to sleep. When Mommy came home from the hospital, she came in and Lil Mason was in the room with Aunt Abigail. She said, "OK, where is my baby?"

We said, "In the room with Aunt Abigail, watching TV."

When she went into the room and saw his head, she was furious. She told Aunt Abigail she was going to whip her tail. Uncle Liam said,

"Hold on there, Ruth Ann." My aunt had jumped out of the bed and into the corner, saying, "Ruth Ann, he looks so handsome," repeating it over and over again. She explained she did the best she could, asking for forgiveness.

My mother said, "He is not even one year old yet. I guess you did your best (saying it in a mean way)." Even though my mother was mad, she let it go, blaming herself for not being there for him. (Aunt Abigail said she was not going to braid another child's head because she had enough heads to do.)

From then on, Mommy would take Lil Mason to the barbershop every other week to get a haircut. Lil Mason would sit in the barber's chair like a big boy. Mommy always took him to get ice cream or give him a piece of candy at the end of it.

O.L. HARRISON

23

MOST OF MY childhood was what I would say roller-coaster time; some were good and others were hard, and this was one of those times that was for me. My mother worked a lot, so she had located a sitter. Various children went to a neighbor who took care of most of the neighborhood children. That was where we experienced a horrible nightmare that would affect us for a long time in our lives. Every day at nap time, our babysitter would leave us with her husband as she would go to the store and do daily chores. He would pick one of us to go into the room with him, saying he needed to check us. I remember him putting me on the bed and taking my underwear to my ankles. He would open my legs and put a blindfold on me before doing this like it was a game. I remember his filthy hands touching me, and I was really scared. He would say, "Don't be scared. I just need to check you, OK?" With fear in me, I would say OK in a scared voice. He would say, "This is just a game, so be sure you are OK, but if you tell anyone," the police would take me from my mother because that was top secret. So none of the children would tell their parents. While this was going on, the other children would be watching the TV.

When his wife would return, she would feed us and then we would take a nap. The sitter and her husband would go in the room together, and we would hear moaning. The babysitter would always say that it was the cat making all that moaning sound.

I don't remember why Mommy stopped taking us there, but I was really glad. Later, the police came to our house, and we had to draw pictures of what we did there. I cannot remember anything else about that time. Cousin Sylvia began to watch us, and Mommy stopped working long hours. I had so much fear (Samantha) in me that I would wet the bed frequently and had bad dreams. I would not go to the bathroom at night by myself, fearing that someone would get me. My mother never talked about this even later in life. All I remember was her saying she was not going to be working long hours anymore.

24

MOMMY WENT BACK to school as she often told us that our education was especially important and that when you finished school, you could have any job you want. No one can stop you from being whatever you want to be. So our mother practiced what she preached and inquired about school. However, to her disappointment, she could not go back to regular school to get her diploma, but she could get her general education diploma (GED). Mommy studied every day even when she went to work. She was amazing, always challenging us to study. She would teach us the things she learned. We would sit down together and do our homework together, sharing her grades, and we share our grades as well. When she completed her GED, we had a big dinner celebration. That was the best time ever. I would say when I grow up, I am going to do things like this with my children. Mommy said, "Except one thing. You are going to finish school and get your diploma before you have children," while smiling. Oh, Mommy said, "Don't forget you have to go to college too, so you can make all that money." Isabella and I laughed.

She taught us what to do and how to have good table manners or good etiquette at the table. She always told us that God is always here for us and telling us the promises of God. God said he would take care of us, which meant that we must do everything that we should do, and he would give us favor with man. She often told us, "Don't trust what people say, and never and, I mean never, allow yourself to be led by someone who is not doing the right things in life. As you have a choice, always choose God. Always pray every day when you get up, bless your food, and every night before you go to bed, ask God for his help and to keep you daily with his loving-kindness and protection. He will. Only you can determine your destination in life, so you have to do the right things for yourself. If you make a mistake, ask God to forgive you, and he will. If you offend someone, be sure to ask them for forgiveness first, then go before God too. Sometimes people will forgive you, and sometimes they will not, but you forgive even if you are right."

These lessons from my mother taught us, I hold true to even this day.

Everything was going well; we were the typical ordinary family, folding clothes, cleaning the house, etc., while often singing or seeing how many clothes we could fold perfectly. Isabella often won the folding clothes game. When we did our chores, Mommy would reward us with a piece of cake, pie, ice cream, or candy. But when we did not do our chores—boy, oh, boy—did we get a spanking. This one time, I knew I was going to get a spanking, so I hid under the bed (a twin bed). When Mommy found me, she lifted up that bed.

"Good gracious." I thought I was going to faint. I was shaking like a leaf. That day, I learned to never hide from Mommy again and to always tell her the truth no matter what.

25

ONE SATURDAY MORNING, someone knocked on the door. It was Cousin Sylvia. All of a sudden, we heard Mommy scream "Oh no!" while Cousin Sylvia was explaining something to her. We heard Cousin Sylvia saying, "Ruth Ann, be strong for the kids," but we could not hear exactly what they were saying. Isabella said that she thought something really bad had happened. I said, "What?" and Isabella said that she didn't know. I said, "I want to finish playing with my papier-mâché dolls."

Isabella said, "Alright. That's grownup stuff anyway."

After Cousin Sylvia left Mommy came into the room and said she had something really, really bad to tell us while putting her arms around us. Isabella said, "What happened, Mommy?"

Mommy paused and gasped for air while blinking her eyes for a moment. "Well, Daddy was really sick, and he died."

The air in the room seemed so thick. Isabella and I began to cry, then Lil Mason cried because we were crying. Mommy said, "We will not be going to the funeral because he was already buried."

Isabella said, "Who buried him?"

Mommy stated, "Just some people." As we continued to cry some more. Mommy sang us to sleep, singing, "Hush, little baby, don't say a word. Mommy's gonna buy you a mockingbird. If that mockingbird won't sing, Mommy's gone buy you a diamond ring," then humming the verses. She held us close to her. That was the longest night of my life. It did not seem like daylight would ever come, waking up at various times during that night.

While we were sleeping, Mommy called her sisters and brother and told them the news about the death of our father. The next day, Mommy said, "We are going on a vacation to Southern Pines this week." We were not going to school that week. Mommy talked to us about God while taking us to the ice cream parlor. Mommy studied a lot of religions because she would state that in all religions, she found some good, but good does not mean God. She studied Presbyterian, Protestant, Muslim, Catholic, Baptist, Jewish, Seventh-Day Adventist, Yahweh, Jehovah's Witness, and even Buddhism. She only stated to us that Buddhism worshipped a statue for their god, and she said that, well, that didn't seem right to her. She was always searching and reading the Bible. She would say, "One day, we are going to find this true and living God." She explained that man was not put here to live forever, but our soul would if we obeyed God.

Isabella asked, "What is a soul?"

Mom said, "It is who you are without your body."

26

THE NEXT DAY when we woke up, Mommy said, "OK, let's go. It's vacation time." Isabella and I were still really sad that Daddy had died. Mommy tried to mask the hurt with fun, but we were still sad. When we arrived in Southern Pines, we stayed with our aunt Sophia and her family. Mommy immediately went looking for a job and a place for us to stay. We returned to New York to complete the move a week later. We were so upset, leaving all of our friends, Yvette and Valerie especially.

While in New York, I hid in the closet, not wanting to leave. I could hear everyone looking for me. Mommy said, "I bet she is in the closet." When she opened the closet door, she was very gentle in telling me that "it's OK, Samantha," as I was crying, "I don't want to go." Mommy said that she understood. "You will meet new friends."

I said, "I don't want any new friends. I want the ones I have."

Mommy then stated, "I know, I know, so you can call them, write them, and we can come back to visit them, and them us." That made me feel a little better. Then she said, "Do you want to go to the ice cream parlor? One more time before we leave? You and your friends can all have some ice cream before we leave."

Isabella said yes. "Samantha, that will be fun."

After going to the ice cream parlor with our friends, we returned to the apartment and finished packing. On our way to North Carolina, Isabella and I played punch cars, and we would look at the clouds in the sky to see the different shapes. Mommy said, "One great day, we are going to see God coming out of the sky. His hand is going to scoop us all up and rescue us."

Isabella said, "Rescue us from what, Mommy?"

Mommy stated, "Rescue us from sin and the bad things that this world holds."

Isabella said, "Mommy, what is sin?"

Mommy said, "Anything that God tells you to do and you don't do, it is sin."

Isabella said, "When does God tell us?"

Mommy said, laughing, "Right now. Now listen to your mother and stop asking so many questions."

I said, "Mommy, I don't hear anything. Do you, Isabella?"

Isabella said, "Not me neither."

Mommy said, "You will learn to hear as you listen quietly and while you read the Bible." That was the turning point for Isabella and me as we wanted to be quiet to hear God speak to us. Then Mommy began to sing, "This is the day. This is the day that the Lord has made. We will rejoice and be glad in it. This is the day that the Lord has made. We will rejoice and be glad in it," repeating the song several times. (I am not sure of the song we sang that day, but this is one she favored singing). We sang ourselves to sleep. Truly, the joy of the Lord is our strength. When we moved, I was twelve years old; Isabella, fifteen years old; and Lil Mason was about two or three years old.

27

F OR FIVE YEARS, everything was well, but around the sixth
year, Mommy was sick again. Some of our family members said
there was a root on Mommy, so they took her to see the root doctor.
The root doctor told them what to do, and the next thing we knew,
my aunt Sophia was in the kitchen, cooking up the strangest stuff you
could imagine—chicken feet, hair from something, blood, and some
other strange stuff. Boy, did that stuff stink up the house! As bad as it
smelled, if that sick spirit did not want to leave, we sure did.

That did not work, and they had to take Mommy back to the
hospital. By that time, we had moved into our own place on Powhatan
Avenue. Our cousin, Priscilla, came to stay with us. Every time Mommy
would come home from the hospital, life would be good. Our cousin
Priscilla was good to us. (We never saw our sisters and brothers from
the other Ruth Ann anymore.) Powhatan Avenue was where my sister
met her husband, Richard Leroy Bailey Jr.

At first, I liked Richard, but my mother said he was too old for
me and introduced him to my sister, Isabella. Isabella and Richard
married. Richard was a great husband, brother-in-law, and son-in-law.
Family was important to him, and he proved that daily. If Isabella's
mother needed money, food, or anything, Richard would do his best
to help out.

Richard's family and ours were good friends, and everyone got along
wonderfully. Life was good. Richard and Isabella had two children,
Cathy and Little Richard. They were adorable. Richard worked at a
local plant, and Isabella stayed home and took care of her children.
Isabella would invite us over on the weekends.

28

MOMMY LATER MOVED to Charles City road apartments. That was where I met my husband, David. When our mother stopped taking her medicine again, a social worker and a nurse practitioner came to our house. They explained what happened to Mommy and what was wrong with her. The nurse explained while illustrating this on a piece of paper that "the brain is like a light bulb. The information went from one part to the other side, and when it connected to the other side, it would make the light come on. But if the line is not connected to the other side, then there would be no light." The nurse explained that if the connection was damaged, the electricity would not get to the other side, and though the light could come on, it would constantly flicker as if it had a short in it. It's like a bridge. To get to the other side you had to cross the bridge; however, if the bridge has a fault in it, then you would not be able to get to the other side without fixing the fault. "Now with your mother's brain, when the information does not get to the other side, it gets scrambled up."

I asked the nurse if they could fix a bridge, then they should be able to fix our mother. She said that they were working on what medicine to give her to fix her. They were trying various drugs to see which one helped her best. At that time, my brother and I were at home together with Isabella, and Richard was checking on us daily as they had a beautiful little girl and lived in an apartment across town.

The doctors finally found a drug to help our mother, and soon she was back at home. She had to take a poliction shot every four to six weeks. She also attended group meetings at a local mental health place. The integrity of the mental health place finally gave us the peace that we needed to help our mother; the kindness and compassion in our situation were felt, and the genuine desire to help us and to understand our mother's illness aided us in dismissing every negative behavior my mother displayed and focused on the good woman that she is.

We also had a wonderful church family, that understood the natural and spiritual things that were going on with our mother. At the local Apostolic Church, the pastor, first lady, and the church people were truly called by God. We had found the same love we had experienced while we were younger. We are truly thankful.

Yes, God is here to heal the family. You might have to search out a matter, but the word of God says, "Seek and you shall find, knock and the doors shall open up." Thank you, God! Always pray! God wants to hear your voice!

We are hopeful that this book will help you understand that thou you may go through hard times and places, God is always there to heal you and your family. We just have to ask, seek, and find. We pray that you find the peace that only Jesus alone can bring in a chaotic world. Blessings.

Made in the USA
Middletown, DE
08 November 2022

14391914R00045